**Power: Or The Story Of Niagara Falls**

**Elbert Hubbard**

In the interest of creating a more extensive selection of rare historical book reprints, we have chosen to reproduce this title even though it may possibly have occasional imperfections such as missing and blurred pages, missing text, poor pictures, markings, dark backgrounds and other reproduction issues beyond our control. Because this work is culturally important, we have made it available as a part of our commitment to protecting, preserving and promoting the world's literature. Thank you for your understanding.

# POWER
## OR
# The Story of Niagara Falls

*By* ELBERT HUBBARD

DONE INTO A PRINTED BOOK BY THE
ROYCROFTERS AT THEIR SHOP, WHICH
IS SITUATE IN EAST AURORA, ERIE
COUNTY, NEW YORK, JULY, MCMXIV

Copyright 1914
By
Elbert Hubbard

# POWER
## Or The Story of Niagara Falls
### By ELBERT HUBBARD

THE Falls of Niagara are one of the wonders of the world.

The Indians called the place the "Thunder of Waters." Father Hennepin, in Sixteen Hundred Seventy-eight, the first white man to view the Falls, spoke of it as the "most inspiring spectacle" that he had ever seen.

The Niagara River is thirty-two miles long, reaching from Lake Erie to Lake Ontario. It is twenty miles from Lake Erie to the Falls, and twelve miles from the Falls to Lake Ontario.

⁋The Falls were once situated at Lewiston, six miles from Lake Ontario, and have gradually eaten their way back six miles.

The progress of the Gorge is well defined and easily followed.

As to the length of time that it has taken for the Falls to make this little journey, there is much dispute.

But, all things considered, there is no doubt that the erosion of the Niagara Falls Gorge is the most valuable aid we have in computing geologic time.

The Falls are possible on account of there being solid strata of limestone resting on soft shale. ⁋The shale is dissolved first, and the overhanging rock gives a perpendicular drop.

If the shale were on top, we would then have simply a rapids.

The limestone varies in depth from twenty-five to one hundred feet, and so the erosion has not always been at the same rate of speed. This is what adds the greatest uncertainty to the age of the Gorge.

Modern geologists seem to agree that it has taken about forty thousand years for the Falls to travel the six miles; and it will take nearly a hundred thousand years for the Falls to reach back to where the City of Buffalo now stands. ⁋ The average potential energy of the Falls is about five million horsepower ∞ So far, the amount of power being used for industrial purposes on both the Canadian and the American side represents a small part of the whole.

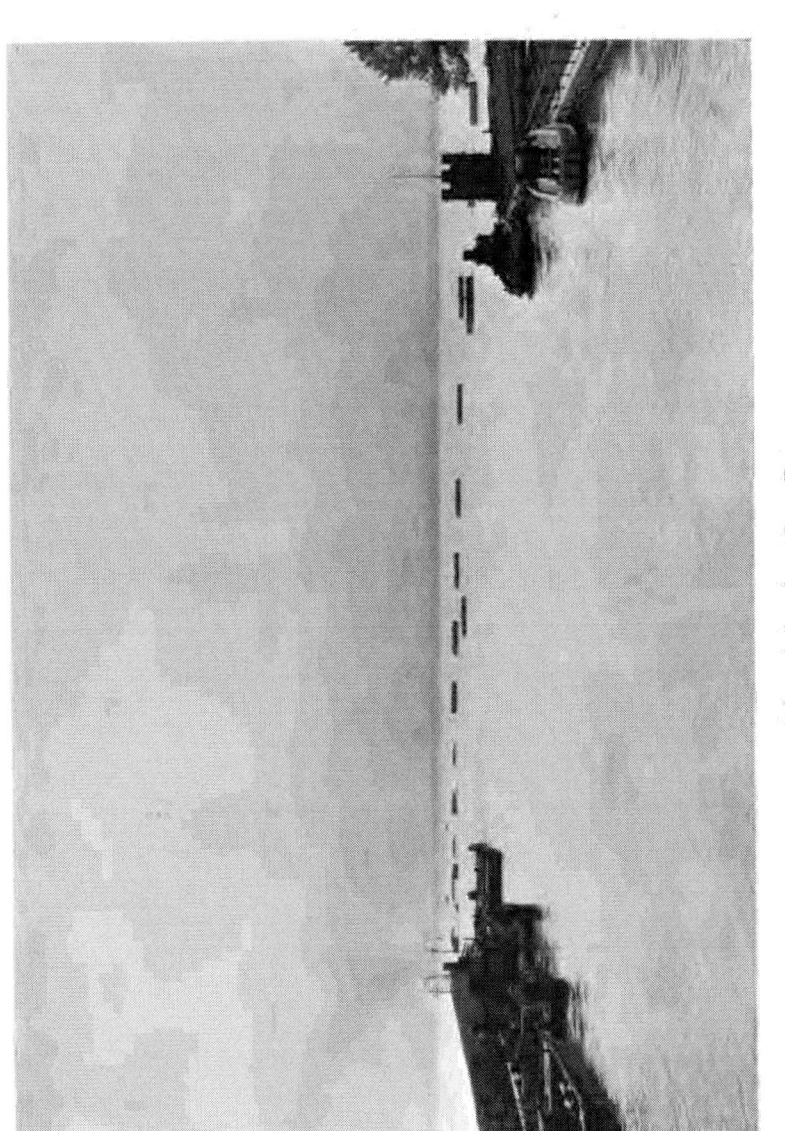

Inlet of Canal at Port Day

Storage Building at Port Day

# NIAGARA FALLS

If all the power at Niagara Falls were used, figuring its value at ten dollars a horsepower a year, we have a total in dollars of fifty million dollars annually.

Should it be proposed to expend fifty million dollars yearly on a spectacle for the people, a mighty chorus of protest would be raised at thought of the extravagance, that would short-circuit the scheme.

Electric power at Niagara is very much below the cost of steam.

## Sentiment

THE objections to using this power instead of allowing it to run to waste are sentimental and poetic, and seem to have come to us from the days of the Indians, who regarded the Falls as a sacred place.

The early explorers told us that the immediate vicinity of the Falls was regarded as neutral ground for all Indian Tribes. Here the Great Spirit had his home, and war was forbidden.

## Pioneers

THE first practical use of the water at Niagara Falls was made in Seventeen Hundred Twenty-five, when a Frenchman built a little canal in the form of a half-circle, just above the Falls. And in this canal he set a waterwheel of his own construction.

It was a crude affair, but it did the work. In fact, as we reckon geologic time by the Niagara Gorge, so can we keep tab on civilization by the way we fail to utilize—or do utilize—the Falls ❧ ❧

The use of the Falls from that time on has developed with the requirements of the people—keeping pace with scientific progress.

From Seventeen Hundred Twenty-five until Eighteen Hundred Six, the only use for the Falls was for running a sawmill.

In Eighteen Hundred Seven, however, a flourmill was established, and to this mill the farmers, from long distances, brought their grists.

Some of them came on horseback; others laboriously carried a hundred pounds of wheat or corn, and carried back flour or meal.

In Eighteen Hundred Twenty-five a paper-mill was added. At that time there were two sawmills and three gristmills, each of these being run by the particular man and his family who owned the mill.

There was no limit to water-rights. The water

was simply diverted from the rapids above the Falls and used in a crude, rude way.

### The Electric Age

THE year Eighteen Hundred Seventy-nine marks an epoch in the onward and upward march of civilization. In that year a Brush Arc Dynamo was installed on the banks of the River.

The electricity generated represented thirty-six horsepower, and this was used for the lighting of Prospect Park.

Excursions were run from Buffalo, Rochester, Cleveland and Toronto to see the wonderful electric lights, and a searchlight was rigged up that added to the wonders of the occasion.

### The Regeneration of the Niagara Frontier

IN Eighteen Hundred Eighty-five the State of New York purchased the little tract known as Prospect Park, and the islands, including Goat Island, in the river adjacent. The purchase was made from the Porter family, who had pre-empted the land and "proved up" on it from the State of New York in Eighteen Hundred Three.

The original Porter estate consisted of a farm

of something like three hundred acres. In the year Eighteen Hundred Fifty-two the Porter family donated to a Company a strip of land one hundred feet wide for the construction of a canal, beginning at a point on the river about one-half mile above the Falls and ending at a point one mile below the Falls.

The intention was to supply power to mills that were to be built along the bank above the Gorge ✒

A day was set apart for the beginning of work on the canal. It was a gala-day, and the whole town turned out to greet this first attempt to utilize the Falls of Niagara in a big and important way.

The village of Niagara Falls at that time contained less than a thousand people.

There were then in Niagara Falls several men who appreciated the fact that any place which was merely a playground, a spectacle, a picnic preserve, would always be poor.

It would be inhabited by guides, hackmen, dealers in curios and souvenirs, and these would constitute a struggling mass of humanity only a few days removed from starvation.

¶ At that time there were Indians who

View of Power Canal Passing Through City

First Hydro-Electric Power-Plant Under High Head

monopolized the curio business, selling little birch-bark canoes, strings of beads, furs and other trinkets.

The people who came to see the sights remained only a day, and Niagara Falls was practically supported by the stray pennies left by these picnickers.

The desire of the Porter family and their neighbors was to produce wealth of a tangible sort by manufacturing raw materials into forms of use and beauty—hence the canal, which was thirty-six feet wide and eight feet deep ✺ ✺

The canal was successfully built, and the waters went dashing around the Fall over the banks of the cliff.

The first power used from the canal was utilized by C. B. Gaskill in the year Eighteen Hundred Seventy-two.

Gaskill dug down in the rock twenty-five feet and diverted a very small portion of the water, dropping it upon a wheel which produced one hundred fifty horsepower.

This mill was in competition with the mills at Rochester which utilized the power of the Genesee River—and it seems that Rochester got the business and the Niagara Falls mill languished ❧ ❧

### Jacob F. Schoellkopf

IN Eighteen Hundred Seventy-seven, Jacob F. Schoellkopf, one of the big businessmen of Buffalo, purchased the canal property and in Eighteen Hundred Seventy-eight formed a new company with the title, The Niagara Falls Hydraulic Power and Manufacturing Company. ¶ A new flourmill was constructed at the top of the cliff, known as the Schoellkopf-Mathews Mill. This was equipped with nine hundred horsepower, secured from big wooden wheels, which soon were replaced with iron. The water was used under a fifty-foot head.

The wheels were nine feet in diameter, placed at the bottom of iron flumes, and these were the first iron penstocks used at Niagara Falls. A little later it was found that a larger drop of the water produced more power, and the Central Milling Company built a flourmill using a head of eighty-six feet.

In Eighteen Hundred Eighty-one, the Niagara Falls Hydraulic Power and Manufacturing Company installed dynamos, and electricity for the first time was supplied to several companies in the vicinity and for the lighting of the city.

These companies were all prosperous; and the successful use of waterpower for producing electricity in a practical way was demonstrated to the business world.

The first wheels put in were smashed to pieces by the fall of the water. It was only after considerable experiment that wheels were made strong enough to withstand the concussion of a vast amount of water falling on them. Pits were dug on the edge of the cliff to depths of from twenty-five to ninety feet. Turbines were located at the bottom of these pits and the water fell to the Gorge below.

## Development

THE Electric Age was upon us, and new discoveries and inventions were being constantly made.

In Eighteen Hundred Ninety-five a new power-station was started, known as "Station Number Two." This station was built well down in the Gorge at the water's edge, and utilized a fall of two hundred ten feet.

So fast have we traveled that the apparatus

in use in Eighteen Hundred Ninety-five for the generation of electricity has practically been abandoned. The scrap-heap has played a big part in scientific developments at Niagara Falls.

Today, in a third and most modern station, there are thirteen separate turbine-wheels, each with a capacity of ten thousand horsepower, all in use. These immense turbines run night and day, being self-lubricating, and built in a way so that friction is practically eliminated.

Concrete with steel has formed a big part in making a very beautiful and secure building that houses the wheels and electric generators.

The first impression is one of astonishment that such a vast power can be developed in so small a space.

The building is at the foot of the cliff.

The water from the canal comes meandering at the rate, say, of three miles an hour. It is diverted through gateways and drops into penstocks or steel tubes two hundred twelve feet upon the wheels beneath. These revolve at the rate of three hundred revolutions per minute.

The penstocks are encased in concrete for

Entrance to Office-Buildings and Power-Station No. 3

The Forebay, Power-Station No. 3

their entire length, so as to provide against possible accidents. Also, there are several safety appliances, so if the pressure of the water gets too severe at any time bursting plates open automatically on the waterwheels and give immediate relief to the penstocks ✒

### An Ideal Manufacturing District

THE Company that owns the cliff and the canal owns also a one-hundred-acre tract of land two miles from the power-station ✒ Upon this tract will be built up in the course of a few years an ideal manufacturing district, not unlike the Central Manufacturing District, which is situated in the exact geographical center of the city of Chicago. There is no reason why manufacturing should be unsightly, unsanitary, or unpoetic in its aspects and attributes ✒ ✒

Business is the supplying of human wants, and in this Hydraulic Power Manufacturing District will be found a series of factories where light, heat and power are supplied from the adjacent Falls carried through cables which run underground.

The equipment is one that will last one hundred years. The great engineers of the world have combined in producing this ideal electric plant.

A short time ago engineers of the United States Government visited Niagara, and the power-plants on the American side were shut down. Measurements of the Falls were taken, both before and after the water was shut off, and so far as the human eye could ascertain the height of the water was exactly the same after as before.

## The Beautifying of the Niagara Frontier

THE first intent of this canal was to supply hydraulic power to the mills that were to be located directly on the cliff.

In the course of time there were a dozen of these little industries where the waterwheels were turned by the weight of the falling water.

The rubbish and refuse from the mills and factories was dumped over the bank, and viewed from the opposite shore the sight was not pleasing.

With the wonderful inventions of Edison came the ability to transform hydraulic power into electric energy, and a new vision was had of the possibilities of Niagara.

The Hydraulic Power Company owns the perpetual right of this canal.

Years ago the State of New York confirmed the riparian rights of this Company and limited the use of water to a canal of a uniform width of one hundred feet and a depth of fourteen feet. The water that flows through this canal every day in the year has a potential energy of at least one hundred fifty thousand horsepower.

The Hydraulic Power Company also owns the high bank from a short distance below the upper steel arch bridge to about a mile below, and the purpose is to employ the very best landscape-artists in the world and make this water-front one of the most beautiful spots to be seen in this country or any other.

### A Model of Efficiency and Beauty

RECENTLY I visited the plant of this great institution, and was immensely impressed with the compactness, beauty and efficiency of the entire institution. It makes one think better of his kind to behold " what man hath wrought."

The real wonder of Niagara Falls will not be seen until the genius of man is combined with

Nature and this vast power is used for the benefit of humanity.

That the Indians should have resented any approach of the whites to Niagara Falls is a thing that we might have anticipated.

And when that first flourmill was placed on the edge of the Gorge, it looked like a transgression. In fact, in Seventeen Hundred Seventy-six, there were only Indians at the Falls, and they passed a solemn law that no white man should even be allowed to live within five miles of the Falls.

The poetic mind of the Indians is still with us. The blend of business and beauty is a new idea. The Indian was solitary. He was a poet. To utilize this wonderful God-given energy for the benefit of humanity was beyond his imagination. He had no mechanical skill.

Building mills on the bank was surely unsightly. Now, however, the cliff has been practically cleared of the unsightly structures that once utilized the Gorge for a dumping-ground.

Beautiful, compact, artistic structures now occupy the space. Down below, thousands of trees have been planted. Vines, flowers, pathways, stairways and all that the genius of architects and engineers can supply in way of beauty, are here to be seen.

The canal in itself, if separated from Niagara Falls, would be a beautiful and awe-inspiring object ॐ ॐ

Man prospers only as he goes in partnership with Nature, reverences Nature, and joins hands with her. We help ourselves by lightening the burdens of the world.

Hydraulic Power Company is inviting many visitors at the Falls to visit its institution and see how water is transformed into electrical energy.

The sight is wonderful, and to me is greater far in its impress than the simple tumbling water over the cliff.

It is a great lesson to children and young people to see how electricity is secured and transmitted, through man's power of invention. If it could be arranged to utilize all of the water at Niagara Falls for industrial purposes for six days in the week, and then, on the seventh, to turn the water on, we would have a spectacle that would attract a far greater number of people than now come here.

Would n't you like to see and study that solid mass of limestone over which the water drops? To walk over the Falls dry-shod will yet be the privilege of mankind.

Then on certain days, advertised far ahead, the water will be gradually turned on, and we will see the Falls for a few hours, just as Father Hennepin saw them.

To liberate mankind from the tyranny of drudgery and the dead lift of labor is the desirable thing.

### *The Schoellkopf Genius*

THE honor of first successfully utilizing the power of Niagara Falls for the benefit of man, in a large way, must go to Jacob F. Schoellkopf.

Others had worked at the idea, but it was the genius of Schoellkopf that made successful use of the power possible. With his prophetic vision he foresaw all the improvements that are now being made, and a good many that it will take years to work out.

Jacob F. Schoellkopf was born in Kirchheim, Germany, in Eighteen Hundred Nineteen. He passed out in Eighteen Hundred Ninety-nine. He was one of the world's greatest workers, and one of the builders of America.

¶ He arrived in this country when he was twenty-two years of age. In two years he had acquired a good working command of the English language.

He located at Buffalo in Eighteen Hundred Forty-four. Starting practically without capital, he built stores, shops, tanneries, mills, and set thousands of people to work.

He erected houses, laid out roadways, managed banks, and, growing rich himself, he made others rich, too.

He had the supreme ability to pick reliable men, and to inspire them with his own animation and ambition.

Schoellkopf possessed in eminent degree the sterling primal virtues for which civilization has never found a substitute—industry, economy, health, good-cheer, truthfulness.

Schoellkopf was a creator of values, a developer of opportunities, a utilizer of the by-product ♣ ♣

Schoellkopf was happily married. His wife was a great help to him in his work, and a deal of the credit for his success should go to her. There were eleven children in the family, eight boys and three girls. These children were all brought up to work, to make themselves useful, to add to the wealth and happiness of the world. They helped themselves by helping other people. And it is now the third generation that controls and operates this wonderful electric plant at Niagara Falls.

Men labor in mines, amid dirt and dust, in darkness and danger, to secure coal that other men may make steam to turn the wheels of trade ৯ ৯

Here at Niagara, Nature in a lavish and bounteous mood has supplied a vast Energy that is only waiting to be harnessed to become the tireless servant of humanity.

For man to use this power and thus lighten labor and add vastly to the wealth of the world, seems not only a privilege, but a duty.

### Triumph of Mind Over Matter

THE world's supply of coal will be exhausted, at the present rate of consumption, in two hundred years.

The supply of iron will be gone in one hundred years.

Three-fourths of the oil-wells in Pennsylvania that once produced, are now dry.

Power-Station No. 3, From Canadian Side

Water-Wheel Room, Power-Station No. 3

A hundred years ago, whale-oil was the one illuminant. Now the whales are gone with the beaver and the buffalo.

In Eighteen Hundred Fifty-nine, Colonel Drake in digging for salt "struck ile."

In Eighteen Hundred Seventy-six, Edison sent a current of electricity through a vacuum, and thereby confounded the Solons who declared there could be no light without combustion, and no combustion without oxygen. ¶ Edison got his light without either, and thereby proved that light was a form of energy, and that energy was transmutable into different forms. ¶ Petroleum is a deposit. It is stored-up fish-oil distilled and preserved in Nature's laboratory. You empty the pocket and exhaust the supply. But electricity is elemental and indestructible. We use it over and over, and like water it traverses earth, trees, animals, clouds, and comes back again to do our bidding. ¶ Water is the natural mate of electricity. They go together. Franklin with his kite and key, coaxing from the skies the secret of electricity, could only work in a thunderstorm. ¶ Electricity has only one love and that is water. And this love is reciprocated.

Mind—human mind—has now evolved so that man, in degree, controls Nature.

And the way he controls Nature is by working with her, never opposing her.

So man can make pyramids and he can remove mountains. He can crumble the hills to dust, transport them to distant points and there reconstruct them.

But in the making of concrete, water is a necessity. Heat applied to water liberates energy, and this was the secret that fashioned the hills and gave form to the mountains. The mighty mixing and explosive power of heat and water is creative.

Creation comes from the currents of electricity exploded by contacts—attraction and revulsion, positive and negative—but always and forever the germ of the unseen becomes visible only when bathed into life by water, and vitalized by a shock.

Well do we speak of "the waters of life." There can be no concrete without water. A man's body is over seventy per cent water. Water is man's most valuable asset, for Nature, as far as we know, can not construct a man without $H_2O$.

And you can not get cheap electricity without water.

The production of electricity as a business is practically in its infancy.

When mankind is delivered from the toil and moil and sweat and travail of unkind conditions, it will be through the utilization of the " current."

We assume there is just one thing in the world, and that is energy. This energy takes myriad forms. Man is the highest product of energy. Call it divine energy, if you wish.

Electricity occupies the twilight zone between the spiritual and the physical.

When Electrical Energy is at last analyzed, dissected, placed on the microscopic slide and weighed on the scales, it will be found to be the very secret of life.

So far, electricity is the jealous secret of Deity. When man becomes worthy, Deity perhaps will share this secret with him. Then indeed will we " be as gods."

Electricity is the passing of power from one form into another. In this respect it is a method of transportation, rather than a thing. The terrestrial program consists of simply two items—absorption and dissipation, receiving and giving, coming and going.

Everything is in motion. Through electricity we transmit energy, dividing it up into units, using it to run a churn, a sewing-machine, a piano, or to produce a heat a thousand times as intense as combustion supplies.

"Do It Electrically!" We certainly are able to do a great many things electrically, but the number of things that we will yet do to advantage electrically, no man can say.

The limit to electrical development, through increased use of electricity and electrical appliances, is absolutely beyond imagination. "The industry is only in its infancy, and our engineers in the kindergarten," says Doctor Charles P. Steinmetz.

Up to this time the education of the public to the use of electricity has been largely a matter of "natural selection"—hit or miss—catch as catch can—now you see it and now you don't.

Electricity, through giving us quick transportation and instant communication, is binding the people of the world together in a common bond. It looks as if the brotherhood

Generator-Room, Power-Station No. 3

Upper Promenade, Power-Station No. 3

of man would not forever be but a barren ideality sung of by poets and prayed for by preachers ❧ ❧

Behind the idea of brotherhood, we now have commercial organization on a broad, generous, far-reaching, friendly plane, with ways and means at its disposal beyond the dreams of avarice. We surely live in great times.

And one thing worth noting is this, while the cost of living has increased, electricity and electric appliances are lower in price today than ever before.

### The Future of the Falls

WE progress through evolution—not revolution ❧ ❧

Electricity makes for advancement; it is a prime factor in the sum total of today's happiness.

Did you ever stop to think of the part electricity plays in your life—of the many advantages and enjoyments you derive, or might derive, from its application to industrial and domestic activities?

By electricity you can run sewing-machines, churns, suction-sweepers, smoothing-irons and laundry machinery.

When you build your new house, have it "wired for service."

Do you ever associate Niagara with your appetite—breakfast-table, the lighting and heating of your home—and thus your health and happiness?

Niagara is intimately connected with these things ♫ ♫

It has made its power felt in trade, commerce and domestic science.

The price of aluminum in Eighteen Hundred Fifty-five—the first year of its commercial existence—was ninety dollars a pound. Now it is thirty-three cents a pound.

Why? Oh, Niagara! that's all.

The aluminum kitchen-utensils in which your coffee is made and your food prepared are by-products of Niagara.

For there is situated the largest plant for the production of aluminum in the world—a plant which produces almost one-half the world's output of that commodity.

Niagara provides the power which permits the perfection of electrolytic methods for the reduction of aluminum. And that so cheaply, that aluminum is rapidly replacing brass and

copper in many departments of industry ❧
Electrical conductors, winding-coils, optical instruments, lithographic supplies, motor parts—these and a thousand and one other uses aluminum is put to.

Confectioners use aluminum boilers in the manufacture of their goods.

And the housewife realizes the beauty, durability and healthfulness of aluminum utensils in the kitchen, and is discarding her pots and pans of iron, tin or enamel.

So Niagara is intimately associated with the ease of the housekeeper.

In Eighteen Hundred Ninety-five a plant of a thousand horsepower was erected at Niagara Falls for the manufacture of a new product—carborundum.

The huge electrical furnaces, which transformed carbon and sand into that wonderful product—which has a range of usefulness extending from the grinding of gems to the hulling of rice in India—were operated by the tireless, resistless, energetic, willing waters of Niagara ❧ ❧

Niagara is the synonym of power. It is the symbol of service. It tokens light—illumination.

Niagara's might gives us light. ¶ It fills huge storage-batteries with the elusive "juice" which we are enabled to utilize at will in our sleeping-cars as we rush across the country on steel rails.

Aye, and erelong Niagara will supply the power that propels trains.

But as yet, we have but touched the fringe of Niagara's possibilities.

Niagara and all of our other great waterways will yet be used, of necessity, for the purposes of light, heat and power, with all the comforts, conveniences and luxuries that man needs for his mental and spiritual unfoldment ❧ ❧

Niagara Falls is wonderful, but the place will not be really worth visiting until the cunning of man's brain has utilized every horsepower of that falling weight for the Service of Man.

¶ I fasten my faith to the Sons of Jove ❧

Promenade in Front of Power-Station No. 3

Building in Lower Factory District

# Interesting Facts About Niagara Falls

**F**IVE power companies are now developing about 450,000 electrical horsepower, equally divided between the American and the Canadian sides of the river. A large supply of power is at a very moderate cost now available.

The descent of the Niagara River, from Lake Erie to Lake Ontario, is 336 feet, of which 216 feet is in the rapids above the Falls and in the Falls themselves, distributed as follows:

|  | FT. |
|---|---|
| From Lake Erie to the commencement of the rapids (21 1-2 miles) | 15 |
| In the half-mile above the Falls | 55 |
| In the Falls themselves | 161 |
| From the Falls to Lewiston (7 miles) | 98 |
| From Lewiston to Lake Ontario (7 miles) | 7 |
| Total | 336 |

Depth of pool from foot of Horseshoe Falls to 2 miles below, 100 to 200 feet.

In Whirlpool Rapids depth averages 50 feet; current 30 miles an hour.

Depth 200 to 300 yards above Cantilever Bridge, 186 feet.

Depth under Cantilever Bridge, 85 feet.

There is no appreciable diminution of the flow of the river as the result of the diversion of water for power development purposes. A flow of one cubic foot per second equals one square mile of water 1.16 inches deep in a 30-day month.

Industrial concerns can locate a plant on each side of the river—one in the United States and one in Canada—and operate the two plants with one executive force, besides being free from tariff complications.

Shipping facilities are unexcelled, with nine trunklines of railroad entering here, and water transportation as well by the Niagara River, Great Lakes and Erie Canal.

Within 500 miles of Niagara Falls 60 per cent of the population of the United States and 80 per cent of the population of the Dominion of Canada reside. New York is less than 500 miles away and Chicago about that distance, while the leading Canadian cities of Toronto, Montreal and Quebec are easily reached by lake and river or by rail.

Over 1,000,000 freight-cars are handled in the joint railroad-yards of Niagara Falls annually.

The value of the annual exports and imports from Niagara Falls, as shown by the report of the United States custom-house, is over $50,000,000. Over 1,100,000 passengers arrive from foreign territory annually. Over 7,300 passenger-trains are inspected. Over 150,000 pieces of baggage are stamped by customs officials annually. Over 4,100 express-cars are sealed for transportation through Canada annually. The number of freight-cars inspected and sealed for transportation through Canada annually is 252,000. The number of entries at the Niagara Falls port is over 26,000 annually.

The estimated investment in power development and manufacturing establishments in Niagara Falls is over $75,000,000.

The number of operatives in industrial concerns in Niagara Falls is over 10,000, with an annual wage of nearly $10,000,000.

Nearly all of the aluminum in the world is made here in three big plants. More abrasive materials are made here than in any other city. There are also large paper and flour mills. Niagara Falls is the chemical manufacturing center of the United States.

The assessed valuation of the city of Niagara Falls for the year 1913 was over $35,000,000, which is about one-half that of the entire county of Niagara.

The number of miles of improved streets is 110, over

41 miles of which have been paved at an expense of over $2,000,000.

The Niagara Falls sewer system cost $1,377,000 and includes 78 miles of sewers.

Niagara Falls has a new municipal water-supply and filtration-plant costing over $1,077,000.

The landed area of the city of Niagara Falls is 6,970 acres, which includes 412 acres in the New York State Reservation at Niagara.

The building permits granted during the year 1912 amounted to over $1,700,000, the greatest building activity in the history of the city.

The New York Central Railroad Company handles over 10,000,000 pounds of package freight per month in Niagara Falls.

The registration in the public schools in Niagara Falls was 4,688 at the beginning of the school year, 1913-14. The total school population, both public and parochial, is estimated to be 7,000. The city has a high school and 12 grade schools.

Niagara Falls has three State Banks, a trust company and a savings-bank, with total deposits of over $9,000,000, and a total capital and surplus of over $900,000.

Twenty-five manufacturing concerns in Niagara Falls reported to the Industrial Commission a product in 1912 valued at $25,000,000.

About 1,500,000 visitors from every part of the civilized world come annually to visit the wonders of scenic Niagara.

The number of farms in Niagara County is 3,044; acreage, 198,598; value, $22,250,957. Hay and grain product of 1909: Corn, 728,478 bushels; Oats, 996,259 bushels; Wheat, 577,082 bushels; Potatoes, 663,192 bushels; Hay, 82,468 tons. Over 1,000,000 apple-trees in Niagara County. Great peach-belt. One of the most important fruit sections in the world.

1 cubic foot of water equals 7 1-2 gallons.

1 cubic foot of water weighs 62.3 pounds.

1 horsepower = 550 foot-pounds per second.

1 horsepower = 1 cubic foot seconds falling 8.8 feet.

$$\frac{\text{seconds feet} \times \text{head}}{11} = \text{horsepower at 80\% efficiency.}$$

The volt is the unit of electrical pressure.

The ampere is the unit of electrical current.

1 volt multiplied by 1 ampere = 1 watt.

The watt is the unit of electrical force.

1,000 watts = 1 kilowatt (Kw)

746 watts = 1 horsepower (Hp)

1 kilowatt = 1 1-3 horsepower.

Niagara Falls power as developed through the hydraulic canal uses 6,500 cubic feet of water per second.

Each cubic foot utilized at Station 3 gives more than 20 E. H. P. or 15 Kw.

Total maximum output 130,000 H. P. or 97,500 Kw.

Efficiency of Waterwheels, 90 per cent.

Efficiency of Generators, 96 per cent.

Printed by Libri Plureos GmbH in Hamburg, Germany